Dog Training

*The Complete Dog Training Guide
For A Happy, Obedient,
Well Trained Dog*

Dan O'Brian

© **Copyright 2015 by _____Dan O'Brian___ - All rights reserved.**

This document is geared towards providing exact and reliable information in regards to the topic and issue covered. The publication is sold with the idea that the publisher is not required to render accounting, officially permitted, or otherwise, qualified services. If advice is necessary, legal or professional, a practiced individual in the profession should be ordered.

- From a Declaration of Principles which was accepted and approved equally by a Committee of the American Bar Association and a Committee of Publishers and Associations.

In no way is it legal to reproduce, duplicate, or transmit any part of this document in either electronic means or in printed format. Recording of this publication is strictly prohibited and any storage of this document is not allowed unless with written permission from the publisher. All rights reserved.

The information provided herein is stated to be truthful and consistent, in that any liability, in terms of inattention or otherwise, by any usage or abuse of any policies, processes, or directions contained within is the solitary and utter responsibility of the recipient reader. Under no circumstances will any legal responsibility or blame be held against the publisher for any reparation, damages, or monetary loss due to the information herein, either directly or indirectly.

Respective authors own all copyrights not held by the publisher.

The information herein is offered for informational purposes solely, and is universal as so. The presentation of the information is without contract or any type of guarantee assurance.

The trademarks that are used are without any consent, and the publication of the trademark is without permission or backing by the trademark owner. All trademarks and brands within this book are for clarifying purposes only and are the owned by the owners themselves, not affiliated with this document.

Just as there are many dog breeds, dog training is just as varied. Unfortunately, many people think that dog training is something done to a dog to make it execute some artificial command. Dog training has much to do with training your dog to be obedient: to obey everything and anything that comes close to him.

Dog training covers a wide range of lessons, which include training your dog new tricks, family manners and many dog skills. Contrary to popular belief, every dog can be trained to a professional level. People assume that training sniffing dogs, service dogs meant for handicapped owners, rescue and search dogs, hunting, carting and sled dogs is a reserve of professional dog trainers. That is not so. In fact, the most highly trained dogs you know are simply carrying out their obedience training to the highest degree. They are trained to behave according to a set of commands that boost their value as helpers to their owner. After training your dog, it will be much more of a pet other than just a wild card. So how do you get started?

TABLE OF CONTENTS

Introduction vii

Chapter 1: Where to Start After Deciding You Want a Dog 1

Chapter 2: Training Your New Dog 9

Chapter 3: How To House Train Your New Dog 13

Chapter 4: Basic Obedience Training 19

Chapter 5: Advanced Dog Training Commands 27

Chapter 6: Socialization Skills 39

Chapter 7: Training Dos and Don'ts 41

Conclusion 47

My Free Gift To You! 49

INTRODUCTION

I want to thank you and congratulate you for purchasing the book, *"Dog Training: The complete dog training guide for a happy, obedient, well trained dog"*.

This book has comprehensive information on how to train your dog.

Having a dog can be one of the greatest things that anyone can ever have. There is a reason why many say that a dog is man's best friend. But just because you got a dog does not automatically mean that you will be the best of friends and have the best of a dog-owner relationship. In fact, if you don't do something to mold your dog the way you want it to be, having a dog can be one of the most frustrating and annoying things you could ever have.

For instance, if you don't train the dog, it might be the kind that never gets off the couch, the kind that poops or pees anywhere and everywhere, the kind that jumps on guests, the kind that cries immediately you put it in the crate, or the kind that you simply cannot fathom going to different places like shopping with. Well, I wouldn't consider that a friend.

Many frustrated dog owners started with the best of intentions hoping that they would have the cute little dog that would accompany them wherever they go without causing ugly scenes like barking at strangers or threatening other dogs. If you have a dog that has some of the annoying habits that you wish it could change so that you can live the life that you've always wanted with your dog, then you need to train the dog to mold its behavior.

There is nothing special about those German shepherds that you see performing some drills that you never thought a dog would do. It all depends on how you train the dog. If you want to transform your dog with proper training, this book will help you to do just that. It will teach you everything you need to do to transform your unruly dog to one that you always adore thanks to its ability to do anything that you want.

Thanks again for purchasing this book, I hope you enjoy it!

CHAPTER 1

WHERE TO START AFTER DECIDING YOU WANT A DOG

Owning a happy, obedient, and well-trained dog is an amazing experience. However, training a dog takes a lot of work and getting started is never easy especially if you have never owned a dog before. Training a dog or puppy takes a ton of work and preparation and with a few unplanned for surprises along the way.

While this may be so, it helps to have some guidance so you can know where to begin when you have made the life changing decision to own a dog. Once you make the decision to buy or adopt a dog or puppy, there are fundamental things you must do to raise and train a happy dog. Below are tips to help you start on the right track as you embark on this fulfilling journey: the journey of being a well-trained dog owner.

1: List Things You Need For Your Dog

Making a list is the best way to break down any difficult task to make it manageable. Likewise, this would be the best way to get started when you have decided to own a dog.

Make a list of the things you will need before your dog comes home, i.e. all the things you need immediately after, and within the first six months of taking your dog home. Doing this will allow you to figure out how much time and money you will need to budget for your dog.

Although you can approach preparation in different ways, here are a few pointers.

Before

Crate; choose a crate that is durable and comfortable. Since crates come in a variety of materials, i.e. fiberglass, wire and heavy molded plastic crate, ask your trainer or veterinarian to recommend to you the best type of crate suitable for your dog.

Note: Some wire crates collapse from easy movements around the house, while molded plastic crates tend to be great for airplane travel in case your dog travels in the cargo bay.

Your crate should be big enough to allow your dog stretching space, as well as turn around and get comfortable space. However, your crate should not be too big. Choose a crate that is fitting for your dog in his or her full-grown size.

Beddings: Choose an easy to clean bedding that is thick enough for comfort.

Water and food bowls: Use ceramic or stainless steel and paint free bowls. Avoid using plastic bowls since they absorbs bacteria and smells.

Flea comb: A flea comb is used as a flea control mechanism.

Brush: Brush your dog on daily basis. It is good for skin and better than bathing.

Pet cleaners: Examples of pet cleaners are; simple solution or nature miracle. They are available in pet supply stores. They remove pet stains and odors.

After

As soon as your dog comes home, it will need an initial check up at the vet's office, tick and flea prevention, and pet insurance if necessary.

If you are a novice, you will need to schedule dog training and obedience classes.

Within the first 6 months of your dog's life, you will need at most three rounds of shots over the first few days and a neuter or a spay appointment.

2: Choosing a Dog

Choosing a dog is more of a compromise than an art. Nevertheless, as a dog owner, you should have a preference beforehand. For instance, do you want a high-energy running dog? Or do you want a small and quiet dog since you live in an apartment? Well, the following are the things you need to consider while choosing what you want in your dog.

The Age You Want Your Dog To Be When Coming Home; by adopting an older dog, you can be able to skip crate and house training, whereas a young puppy will need some training, which will have a greater impact on how your dog's behavior is molded and shaped.

The Size of The Dog You Want: the bigger the dog, the more it eats and the more space it needs. Some people like big dogs especially if they're living alone and want to feel protected.

Are You Ready To Train Your Dog? If yes, you need to consider the breeds of dogs that are easier to train. Some breeds are difficult to train than others. Some of the easy to train breeds include Labrador Retriever, Australian Shepherd, Belgian Sheepdog, Poodles, Golden Retriever,

Australian Cattle Dog, Border Collie, German Shepherd, Doberman Pinscher and Bloodhounds.

3: Figure out Which Breeds Fit Your Lifestyle

Every dog breed has its own popular characteristics, starting from high energy to being tough to train. Therefore, you need to spend some time doing research on different dog characteristics in relation to breeds. You can use sources such as [Animal Planet Dog Breeder](#) selection or [American Kennel Club](#) to gain some insight into your preferred dog characteristics.

Sometimes, you may get overwhelmed by a dog breed you barely know. Research will help you get the most out of it and make sure you approach choosing a dog from a knowledgeable point about what you might be looking for in terms of personality.

4: Where to Find Your Dog; Breeder vs. Shelter

While opinions are divided between choosing a dog from a breeder or shelter, you will find that one of them is the best for you. However, the truth is that at the end of it, a lot has to do with the individual than it does with the dog. The decision to choose from a breeder or a shelter is often a heavy one for most new dog owners.

Breeder-With breeders, you will find it much easier to control the outcome, which tends to be great for the novice dog owners or the experienced dog owners who has particular needs and preferences.

Dogs found in breeders come home with only the first round of vaccination but they have fewer cases of dog abuse or troubled pasts. If you opt to go with the breeder option, it is highly recommended that you buy your dog from a responsible dog breeder such as a [Kennel Club](#).

Shelter-shelter dogs are wildcards. In many cases, you will not know more about a sheltered dog's past in terms of abuse or neglect the dog may have suffered before.

If you have researched the kind of breed you want and are not sure of the breed to go for, or feel the need to check out the various breeds from somewhere else other than internet, a shelter is an ideal place.

Sheltered dogs are likely to be vaccinated, spayed, and sometime micro chipped.

5: Picking Up Your Dog

When picking up your dog, try to find out the kind of diet the dog eats to avoid stomach problems. Stick to that meal plan for the first few days. In case you want to switch to a different type of food, do it over a period of one week by adding one portion of new food to three portions of the previous meals.

In rare cases, some dogs find car trips stressful. In this case, secure your dog in a crate to make the journey a bit easier and safer. Immediately after bringing your dog home, take them to the toilet area of the house, and spend some time with them there to get the dog accustomed to that area and use it to relieve themselves.

Next, place your dog on a leash and walk it around the house. Since your dog might be anxious about this new place, don't be surprised if the dog exhibits insistent pacing and panting, excessive drinking, house training accidents and chewing or gastric upset. A male dog that was not neutered early might mark the new territory especially if you have other pets living there. Give your dog enough space to settle down to avoid your new dog being overwhelmed.

Next, take your dog to its crate. Take your time to encourage your dog to sniff around, and reward him with small treats for entering the crate. Put some soft beddings and safe toys in the crate and leave him to relax.

6: Naming Your Dog

Naming your dog is the first step towards developing a close bond between you and your dog. However, coming up with a companion's names may be harder than you think. Below are tips to help you pick your dog's name.

Keep It Short, Crisp and Sweet

While naming your dog, limit its name to one or two syllables, just to make sure that your dog can easily understand it. Long dog names will only confuse your dog, since lengthy names are incomprehensible to the canine due to their long weird sounding wordings and intonations.

Try Out Names with Sharp Consonants

Dogs are good at hearing sounds with high frequency; names starting with s, ch, sh, etc., are good at catching a dog's attention. These sharp names will enable your dog to respond quickly compared to other names. Further, consider names that end with long vowels; this can be a short "a" or a long "e" sound, i.e. Kassie, sweetie, samba, Charlie, or Delilah.

Never mix dog commands like "down", "sit", "come", with the name of your dog. This causes confusion and your dog might not respond correctly. For instance, "bit", and "sit", or "fay" and "stay"

DOG TRAINING

Stick to Similar Sounds While Renaming an Older Dog

Be cautious when you want to change an older dog's name. Stick to a similar name as the previous one. For example, changing "barney" to "Farley", it's crucial to maintain the vowel sounds similar than the consonants, because dogs pick up vowel easily and that what he listens to. i.e. "pinky" will go along with "Mikey" but not "Pokey".

CHAPTER 2

TRAINING YOUR NEW DOG

Every dog should be trained. Your dog should know basic manners, important things and a few tricks. After you bring your new dog home, you will be ready to start training. To maximize your dog's learning potential and ensure you are both enjoying the training classes, keep the following tips in mind.

Training Tips for New Dog Owners

Keep Training Sessions Sweet And Short: whenever you are teaching your dog new skills, it tends to be like a young child. Dogs do not have long attention spans. While there is no hard and fast rule in dog training, an ideal dog training session should not exceed 15 minutes.

During a single session, you can choose to introduce one new skill or switch between a few different skills. To keep your training interesting, try to do 5-15 repetitions of similar behavior followed by 5-15 repetitions of another behavior.

You can also introduce new skills to your dog and improve the old ones by doing single repetitions at suitable times during the day. For instance, before serving your dog meals, ask him to sit or lie down first.

Before the end of a training session, quit on a good note by ending it with a skill you know your dog is good at. This will ensure you have ended the session without either one of you getting bored, tired, or frustrated.

Note that dogs were not born with an understanding of English. They can only learn significant words such as, walk, sit, treat etc. If you combine these familiar words with complex sentences, your dog will get confused. For instance, you might confuse your dog by saying "fluffy down", then another day you say to your dog, "sit down" "fluffy". If you do this, you might wonder why fluffy does not act the same way every time. While teaching your dog a command or cue, choose just one phrase or word that you will consistently be using all through.

Take baby steps. Dogs are similar to us in many ways. For example, dogs learn better when new tasks are broken down. When introducing a new skill, start with easy steps and increase difficulty as you proceed. For instance, when you are training your dog to stay, begin with 3 seconds stay, then increase the stay to a duration of 8 seconds. After your dog has mastered the 8-second stay, make things a bit harder by increasing the time to 15secs, 30secs, etc. This will make your dog learn faster.

Work on one particular skill at a time. Most of the skills you want your dog to learn are complex. For example, if you want your dog to learn a solid sit-stay, you should teach him to stay in a sitting position until you release him. This can be; he should stay until you move from him or stay until things around distract him. If you teach your dog different skills at the same time, you and the dog might end up frustrated. Instead, start with one skill, and after mastering that skill, introduce another.

For instance, work on duration first. When he can stay-sit for a few minute in a quiet place that has no distractions, stand next to him, start training him as you move away from where he is. Focusing on that new skill, go back and ask him to sit for a while. Stay around and build up the duration of the stay again. Proceed by training him in a more distracting place. Gradually proceed by making the skills harder and harder but in an easier way. At the end of it, your dog will have mastered everything.

When you run into trouble, go back a few steps. If you introduce a new skill to your dog and fail to see any progress, you will have increased the level of its difficulty too quickly. In this case, refresh his memory by making a few repetitions. Start from the skill you know your dog can perform well and practice for a while without adding to the difficulty.

Practice the learnt skills everyone and with anyone. Dogs tend to learn very specifically and do not apply what they learnt in different situations, people, and places. If you teach your dog to stay in kitchen, he will be a kitchen-trained dog. However, ask him to sit at a different locations and he might not understand what you mean. For him to perform his skills everywhere, practice skills at different places; your yard and home, in the street, at a friend's place or at the park.

Use real rewards. Get used to rewarding your dog with things he finds truly rewarding. You will find that some dogs will happily train in your room and ignore the training while in the park. This might be because the park is very distracting which makes it hard for him to pay attention to the training sessions.

Pay your dog according to the reward that is worth working for. This can be bits of chicken or cheese, or a chance to run off-leash with his friends at the park. Note that the reward might change at a given time. If he has eaten his meal, a scratch behind his ears would be more rewarding than chicken and cheese. If he has not eaten for some time, then a reward based on bites would be worth.

Be persistent. Training your dog might take you some time and effort. Take it slow, and with time, you and your dog will accomplish great things.

CHAPTER 3

HOW TO HOUSE TRAIN YOUR NEW DOG

House training an adult dog or a puppy may appear daunting, but every dog can be trained how to eat, play, sleep, relieve himself outside and so on. It is up to you as a dog owner to teach your dog responsible behavior that go along with your requirements.

Note that punishing your dog has never been a remedy to bad behavior. Instead, punishment only scares away your dog. A good sense of humor and patience are the key to helping your dog adapt to life as a pet. Below are three easy ways to house train your new dog.

Setting up A Routine

The first thing to factor in while house training your new dog is coming up with a routine. Here is how it goes…

1: Take Your Dog Outside Frequently

Taking your dog outside time after time is one of the crucial things to do while teaching your dog to relieve himself. While it may appear to be excessive, take him outside as frequently as possible, about every half an hour. Stick to this schedule and try not to miss even one chosen "outside" time so as your dog can associate this outside time with relieving himself.

In case you are training a puppy, take him outside more frequently because puppies have small bladders and can't hold their pee for long.

2: Put Your Dog on a Feeding Schedule

Get into a routine of feeding your dog at the same time in the morning and at night. After the meals, wait 20-30 minutes before you take him outside. A feeding schedule will help you predict when your dog needs to go to the bathroom, hence making house training a bit effortless.

For a puppy, create a three-meals-per-day feeding schedule bearing in mind that he needs to be taken outside more frequently.

3: Learn To Interpret Signs That Your Dog Has To Go

These signs include; walking around stiffly, holding its tail in a funny position, sniffing the floor as if he is looking for something and so on. Once your dog shows the signs that he wants to pee or poop, take him outside immediately even if it's before the outside time.

Include verbal cues like saying "outside" before you take him out. Eventually, you will be in a position to ask him if he needs to go outside by saying the word.

4: Choose a Specific Spot Outside

Choose a specific place where you will be taking your dog each time you take him out. This can be somewhere in your backyard or close to a green patch of grass. Dogs are creatures of habit. When he gets used to this spot, it will be his most comfortable place to pee each time he goes outside.

Once you reach the spot you have designated, use a verbal cue such as "go potty". This will help him associate relieving himself with the place.

5: Keep Your Dog In A Crate At Night And When You Are Away

If you leave your dog free to roam the house during the night, he might end up soiling the floor. To avoid this mess, keep him in a comfortable crate at night and when you are not around. Dogs dislike soiling their dens, so he will have to wait until he can go out to relieve himself.

Note that dogs should see their crates as their safe place and should enjoy spending time there. In this case, don't keep your dog in the crate as a form of punishing him. When you use it in that manner, he will associate the crate with fear instead of comfort.

Also, don't let your dog stay in the crate for too long before going outside. If he does, he will have no choice other than relieving himself in there. Your dog will need plenty of exercises, and play time, so he should be in the crate for no more than a few hours or overnight.

6: Clean Up Messes Immediately

If your dog makes a mess indoors, which tends to be normal, clean it up instantly and use a cleaning solution to get rid of the smell. In case your dog smells old mess at a particular spot, he will think of that place as a potty spot.

Don't punish your dog when they make a mess; simply clean it up and get back to the schedule.

Rewarding Your Dog For Good Behavior

Did you know that dogs need to be rewarded after every single time they stick to a particular good behavior? Yes! Your dog will do anything to get a reward! Take advantage of that by rewarding him anytime he does it right. Below are some of the cases you will need to reward your dog after setting up a routine…

1: Give Your Dog Praise and a Treat Every Time He Goes Outside Successfully

Your dog will learn best through positive reinforcement and he will quickly learn the best way of achieving it. Each time your dog uses his designated spot in the right way, reward him with lots of praises, a little treat and a scratch on the head.

You need to be consistent when it comes to rewarding your dog. Do it every time he goes to the potty in the potty spot and after learning all the other good behavior.

2: Time Rewards Correctly

When treating your dog for using his potty spot correctly, do it once he relieves himself. Don't do it too early or too late because he will not associate it with relieving himself in the right spot.

3: Consider Using a Chime or a Bell to Aid in Training

Some people attain dog-training success while using the bell method instead of a treat. After your dog relieves himself in the potty spot, ring a bell or a pleasant-sounding chime as a way of rewarding him. Your dog will look forward to the sound of the chime.

4: Keep Your Tone and Manner Light and Friendly

Each time you are taking your dog to the potty or talking about it, keep your voice pleasant and light. Do not raise your voice or talk in a harsh tone, because your dog can take his bodily functions as a punishment and associate it with fear. If he messes indoors, withhold the praise instead of yelling at him.

When you are using verbal cues like "go potty", "outside", or "good dog" be consistent. Repeat these words along with the environment and actions to reinforce where you want him to relieve himself.

Paper Training Your Dog in an Apartment

Were you worried whether you can still adopt a dog in an apartment? Well you can. Here is how to train your dog to be well mannered even when he is indoors most of the time.

1: Choose an Out-Of-The-Way Spot That Is Easy For Your Dog to Access

If your house is located in a high rise, it almost impossible to make it outside every time your dog wants to relieve himself. Instead, pick a spot inside your house that is not right in the middle of your living room but also easy for your dog to access at any time. This can be a corner of the laundry room or kitchen. Let the spot be in a hard wood or vinyl flooring space instead of a carpet.

2: Line the Designated Spot with Training Pads or Newspapers

Newspaper is affordable material you can use while creating a potty for your dog. If you choose to use the absorbent training pads, you can find them in pet stores.

You can as well use a dog litter tray. In case you want your dog to adopt reliving himself outdoor and indoor, fill up the tray with soil for the dog to associate that as an acceptable area to relieve himself.

3: Change The Mat Often But Leave A Small Spot Of Dried Urine On There

As said earlier, old urine smell will remind your dog that the mat is the place to go potty. Get rid of feces right away but leave a small spot of paddling or newspaper with urine on the clean mat so your dog will know the place to go.

4: Reward Your Dog for Going in the Right Spot

Every time your dog relieves himself on the mat, reward him with petting, praise and a treat. He will associate going potty in the mat with the positive feeling, and eventually, he will start going there without help.

CHAPTER 4

BASIC OBEDIENCE TRAINING

Trying to control your dog before learning obedience commands is tiresome and almost impossible. However, teaching him 5 basic commands will make a world of difference and provide a great chance for bonding.

Note that puppies have short attention spans. It is unreasonable to expect your puppy's attention to last for long periods. In this case, keep your sessions short and increase the duration gradually.

The Sit Command

The sit command is one of the easiest skills to teach. A dog that sits on command is easier to manage before he learns more self-control. For instance, if you teach your dog to sit when the doorbell rings, there will be minimal chances of him jumping on visitors when the door opens.

How to teach sit

1. Get on the same level with your puppy, either on the floor or in a chair next to him.

2. Hold a treat next to his nose and let him follow the treat as you move your hand up.

3. While his head moves up, his butt will lower down.

4. After his butt hits the floor, place the treat in his mouth and instantly praise him for his intelligence and obedience.

5. Repeat this multiple times every day. Pair this behavior with the word "sit." Avoid holding the treat too high that the mutt has to jump for it. Rather, hold it in a position where he will have to stretch his neck. Immediately his rump hits the floor, tell him, "Good sit".

6. Repetitions tend to be crucial. However, your dog will get tired of multiple repetitions. To avoid that, play the sit game in short bursts several times throughout the day. Reinforce the sit command in other situations such as mealtimes.

7. Ask him to sit before putting his bowl of food on the floor, or before you open his door while taking him out for a walk. If he breaks the sit command, remind him with simple word like "oops. Try again".

The Come Command

Come command is one of the most useful tools for managing an annoying behavior in puppies. This command is used to help your dog get out of trouble or when giving him some work to do. You will use and refine this foundation skill for the rest of your dog's life.

How To Teach Come

1. Clip a light line on your dog's collar, then allow him to drag it around.

2. After he is familiar with the line, pick up one end and hold it as you follow him around. While he gets used to this, he will begin to realize that both of you are attached.

3. Keep the marker word in mind – "yes" – and a few treats, turn and walk backwards motivating him to follow along. After he twirls around and comes towards you, tell him "yes" with a treat.

4. Pair this behavior with the word "come". Each time he responds correctly, reward and praise him. Make this a game that he will enjoy playing.

5. Avoid yelling, "come, come, come, come," in case your dogs does not respond. Keep in mind that it is a one-word command and a one-word rule. However, when your dog understands the come command and after calling him he does not show up, you will have to gently guide him to where you want him to be.

6. When your dog is not responding to your command, it's either he does not understand or you are expecting too much from him.

Note: Never call your dog to come for discipline. If you do so, he will associate the come command with negative consequence. If you want to discipline your dog, go right to where he is instead of calling him.

The Stay Command

The stay command tends to be harder to learn for both young dogs and puppies. Asking a comfortably sited dog to move and stay somewhere else is almost asking for too much.

Just like any other command, the stay command is a lifesaver. A dog taught how to stay will never chase ducks in yards or charge at cows in the field. When your dog understands the stay command, he can participate in advanced obedience tricks or rally contests.

The stay command aims to teach a dog to remain still wherever he is until the further notice.

How to Teach Stay

1. Put a leash on your dog and sit comfortably next to him.

2. Waving a flat palm towards his muzzle, say, "stay".

3. Move in front of your dog for a few seconds, and then move back beside him.

4. Praise him for not breaking his stay.

5. In case he moves, calmly say "uh uh" or "oops" and take him back to the initial place. Again, give him the stay command together with the hand signal.

6. Practice this severally during the day in different locations

7. After you have rewarded him for the success, teach him words that will let him know when he is released from the stay. A nice release word is "okay".

The Down Command

The down command is an essential skill in managing your dog, keeping him out of trouble, and getting him out from underfoot. This skill tends to be a bit hard for some dogs because it is a submissive posture. A fearful or shy dog finds it hard to learn or perform the down command.

Note: It is very important that you go slowly while teaching your dog this skill and use lots of praise, and a happy, pleasant voice while teaching your dog this skill.

How to teach down

1. Hold a very pleasant treat in your hand and enclose it within your palm. Place this arm near your dog's muzzle.

2. After he notices the smell of the treat, start moving your hand towards the floor somewhere in front of him. His body will follow his head stretching out into a down. When he does, open your hand and give him the treat.

3. Repeat this several times daily and pair it with the word "down".

4. In case your dog lunges towards your hand, say "nope" and move your hand away before he gets to the treat. If he tries to sit up instead, break away and start again.

Note: Never try to push your dog into sitting down.

Encourage your dog for every bit of progress achieved until he completely understands the command. Often release him from the down and continue with other games.

The Walk Nicely On Leash Trick

A dog who does not pull or lunge at the end of his leash indicates he is a well-trained pet. A dog well trained to walk besides his owner is less likely to become fearful in new situations.

How to Teach Walk Nicely On Leash

1. Clip the leash to the buckle collar and using a happy voice to say, "let's go". Place treats in your bait bag or your left side pocket.

2. Encourage him to move forward by patting your left leg. Whenever he comes close to your side, pop a treat in his mouth.

3. After every few steps, stop praising him for being in the correct position.

4. If he lags behind or forges ahead, stop moving to let him wander to the end of his leash.

5. The slight tension on the leash will probably make him to turn around. Immediately after, you feel the leash slacken, utter the verbal praise word, "yes", followed by a treat and praise after he bounces back to you.

6. If he pulls, stop moving and he will auto correct his unwanted behavior. Then wait for him if he does not come back to your side.

Note: Loose-leash walking is best done if you are an active owner who is patient enough to teach his dog proper behavior even after making a hundred mistakes.

Once your dog starts walking on a loose leash, start to pair the behavior with the "heel" command that means, "stay close to my left leg whether we are walking or have stopped."

After you take a few steps with your dog in the heel position, praise and treat. Keep on practicing until your dog learns this command.

Note: Dog training is a continuous process; you just don't stop at teaching your dog basic commands. That's why you will need to advance your training to teach your dog a few advanced dog training commands to make you a cool dog owner. By teaching him or her some of the advanced commands, you will definitely feel more proud and cement your relationship with your dog. You can be sure that you will benefit a lot more from your best-friends-for-life relationship with your furry friend! Let's learn some of the advanced commands that you can teach your dog in the next chapter.

CHAPTER 5

ADVANCED DOG TRAINING COMMANDS

The Speak Command

Teaching your dog the speak command develops your dog's communication skills. The speak command teaches your dog to bark when he or she wants to get your attention. This is helpful because it helps your dog get used to the idea of speaking, which in this case means barking, whenever he needs to go outside.

You can also use the speak/bark signal to train your dog to alert you when there is a stranger nearby, when it is hungry, when its water bowl is empty, or when it wants to come back to the house.

How to Teach Speak/ Bark

1. Take a leash or a long line, and attach it to something secure such as a tree or fence.

2. Attach your dog by his wide buckle collar or a harness to the tie down.

3. Tie his toy on a short pole with a stick.

4. Dangle the toy back and forth in front of your dog making sure the toy remains out of reach.

5. Out of the frustration, your dog will bark at the toy.

6. When the dog barks, ensure to reward him by letting him or her to grab and even play with the toy for a short moment and then proceed to ask him to 'drop it'.

7. Continue doing this until the dog can bark regularly on command.

8. Add the 'bark command' and if the dog barks on command, offer some reward and positive reinforcement.

9. You can also teach your dog a hand signal once it has learnt to bark on command.

10. Show it the hand signal as you say the command.

11. After your dog masters the speak command as well as its adjacent hand signal, opt to use the hand signal instead of the verbal command.

The Quiet Command

One of the easiest ways to stop your dog from barking is to teach it the quiet command. You don't want your dog to start barking when you are in the middle of an important conversion or when you don't want to attract too much unnecessary attention. As long as you are in control of it, barking is a fine behavior in dog. It would be great to only let the dog to bark when you truly want it to bark as opposed to any other time.

How to Teach the Quiet Command

1. Encourage/wait for your dog to bark.

2. Allow your dog to bark a couple of times before showing it a tasty treat. Calmly utter the command word "quiet." Don't shout or be exited. Be calm and stay in control. When your dog catches the sight

of the treat, it will focus its attention on it and stop barking.

3. If it remains quiet for 5-10 seconds, reward it.

4. If it starts barking before the 10 seconds, don't reward it.

5. Attempt the exercise again in a couple of minutes, this time rewarding it for remaining silent for 5 minutes.

The Wait Command

If your dog is highly energetic, you must teach it the wait command. The wait command tells your dog where he must stay until you let him know he can move. You can use this command in conjunction with the stay command but both are individual commands with different meanings to your dog.

How to Teach the Wait Command

1. Start by teaching your dog to wait patiently at the door. Place a leash on the dog and it ask it to sit.

2. Reach for the doorknob as soon as its rear touches the ground.

3. It will instantly get up. As it does so, pleasantly say 'Oops!' then take your hand away from the knob, and ask the dog to sit.

4. Reach for the doorknob again and the dogs makes to stand again, say 'oops' and take your hand away from the door.

5. Your dog will get the idea after a few trials. When the idea sinks in, challenge it by taking it outside.

How to Teach Wait Outside

1. Still on a leash, walk your dog near an obstacle such as a bridge, a flight of stairs, or the door.

2. Say the word 'wait' in a firm tone, as you move towards the obstacle while holding the leash taught.

3. If your dog stops and looks at you, praise it and give it a treat.

4. If it continues, give it a gentle tug on the leash and repeat the command. Say 'No, wait' in a more firm tone.

5. When your dog has successfully waited for a short time, let your dog know that it's ok to continue on by saying 'Ok.'

6. Repeat this exercise until the dog is responding immediately to the word 'wait.'

The Leave It Command

When your dog knows and understands the leave it command, it will give you peace of mind knowing that you can effectively control the dog. How cool would it be when you don't have to worry about having to monitor your dog's every little movement even in an environment where there are nice treats?

How to Teach Leave It

1. Place your dog on leash, under control, and he cannot get to the object you are going to ask them to leave it. Choose something neutral that does not excite or bore your dog.

2. Place the item within the dog's sight; when he makes a grab for it, tell the dog to leave it; when the dog completes your command, click the training clicker, and give the dog a treat.

3. Repeat this 4-5 times.

4. Repeat the process with something your dog likes but does not love, and again, tell the dog to 'leave it.'

5. If the dog tries to take the object, pull back the object until it learns to ignore it.

6. Practice this exercise repeatedly until your dog willingly follows it command and ignores his favorite toy. Continue practicing with more challenging objects until the command sinks in.

7. Move your training outside where you can teach your dog to ignore other dogs, squirrels, and people. Click and reward every time your dog obeys.

The No Command

This command teaches your dog to stop doing what s/he is doing or s/he won't have something. You can use this command to stop the dog from engaging in unwanted behaviors such as jumping on you or someone else, chewing, or biting. This basic command will help you keep your dog well mannered.

How to Teach the 'No'

1. Teach this command when your dog is not full, but hungry enough to be attentive. Have several different kinds of treats that your dog really likes in your hand.

2. Hold one of those treats flat in your closed hand 6 inches from the dog's mouth.

3. Your dog will naturally try to grab it. Quickly say the word 'No!' in a firm tone, and quickly enclose the treat in your fisted hand.

4. If the dog fails to stop, simply pull your hand away from the dog until he resets and remains calm.

5. Place your open hand again at the dog's eye level about 6 inches from the mouth.

6. Once again, when the dog makes for the treat, quickly close your hands into a fist while saying 'No.' Repeat this process for 5 minutes then give it a five minutes break to reset the brain.

7. After 5-10 sessions, your dog will have grabbed the concept.

Note: Be quick to withdraw your hand. Your dog can be sneaky when it sees your hand open.

The Heel Command

The heel command helps you control your dog when on a walk, and when you are around other dogs or people. The heel command places your dog on your side instead of pulling on his leash.

It is a formal obedience exercise where your dog learns to walk by your knee, matching your pace and sitting down when you halt. This way, you will have better control of him should you meet another person or dog.

DOG TRAINING

How to Teach Heel

1. Begin your lesson when your dog is in a calm frame of mind.

2. Place your dog on a leash. If this excites the dog, wait a few minutes until the dog calms down. Pick the leash up and begin to walk.

3. Offer your dog a treat to entice him to walk besides you, and offer it plenty of praises once your dog starts moving with you.

4. If it pulls on the leash and jumps ahead and starts pulling on the leash, stop and wait until it has stopped tugging and pulling.

5. Simply stand, patiently wait, and ignore your dog; do not yell or pull at the leash, simply hold a tautly.

6. Once your dog calms down, call him or her back and offer rewards, praise, and treats when he does as instructed.

7. Once you and your dog are moving together, say the word 'heel' repeatedly.

8. If your dog jumps ahead, stops, or lags behind, entice him or her back to your side, and begin again.

9. When your dog walks next to you when you utter the heel command, reward it with plenty of praises and an occasional treat.

10. Progressively practice this exercise in your home, then slowly extend the distance, switch the directions frequently, and remember to give your dog plenty of praises every time he or she follows the heel command.

The Stand Command

This command comes in handy at bath time or grooming time. It is a must teach command for any dog owner. So how do you make your dog to stand on command?

How to Teach Stand

1. Ask your dog to sit in front of you, about a foot away.

2. Hold a treat parallel to its nose, a few inches away and slowly move the treat forward towards you.

3. As your dog stands to reach for the treat, praise, and quickly give it the treat as a reward.

4. As it stands, offer the treat, use the stand signal, and praise your dog.

5. Practice this several times a day.

6. Once it is standing quickly with the hand signal, add the verbal cue "stand."

The Off Command

Even if you're comfortable with it, others might find it uncomfortable when your dog jumps on them. This command teaches your dog to stay down and not to jump up on you or anyone else. It also keeps your dog off the furniture.

How to Teach Off

1. Have your dog sit in front of you; in front of its nose, hold a treat the dog considers yummy. Don't allow your dog to grab the treat. Just let it sniff it.

2. As it paws at the treat and shows frustrations to get it, firmly give the verbal command 'Off!' without yelling.

3. As soon as it makes the slightest movement from your hand with its nose, give it the treat and praise it.

4. Practice the command using 5-15 seconds sessions several times a day.

The Jump Command

This command teaches your dog to jump in the air with all four paws off the ground, but not over objects. If you want to be the coolest dog owner in your neighborhood, this is definitely something that you want to teach your dog. There mere sight of your dog jumping on command will simply be amazing. So how do you teach your dog to jump on command?

How To Teach Jump

1. Get your dog exited.

2. Grab your touch stick and hold it closer to the ground so that your dog has to jump up to touch it.

3. Click, and treat your dog as soon as its legs are off the ground.

4. Raise the touch stick higher and let it jump again. Click and reward once it jumps.

5. Gradually push your touch stick higher and introduce the verbal word 'jump' every time it jumps. Keep praising and rewarding every time it jumps over.

6. Keep doing this until he eventually jumps at your command.

7. Stop using the touch stick and use your command instead. Click and treat whenever he does this.

The Drop Command

Your dog will use its mouth to pick up something that might be unhealthy/harmful for it. Dogs often swallow safety pins, needles, and other small objects before you can retrieve them.

The drop command will save you and your dog from the risk of injury. This command makes playing fetch more fun when your dog returns with ball and drops it at your feet or in your hand for another toss.

How to Teach Drop

1. Gather 3 items, a toy your dog likes, the one it loves, and some treats your dog likes.

2. Choose a quiet place free from interruptions

3. Give your dog a toy that it likes and allow it to play freely.

4. Give the 'drop it' command when you are ready. Say this command only once.

5. Then move the tasty treat slowly right in front of your dog's nose.

6. As soon as the dog drops the toy, ensure to praise and then treat it.

7. Repeat this exercise at least 5 times the first time you do it and a couple of times thereafter.

8. After about a week of practice, give your dog a toy they love instead of the one they like.

9. Repeat the same procedure replacing the toy with a treat. Before advancing the game again, revert to an item your dog likes less if he fails to drop the item.

10. Stop giving your dog a treat every time it follows through.

11. Continue repeating the exercise with progressively more challenging toys and treats. Every time something is in your dog's mouth is an opportunity to train the drop it command by asking the dog to 'drop it' and praising and treating him/her whenever they do it.

The Fetch Command

Playing fetch is a great way to have fun with your dog, and exercise him at the same time. A dog can be very particular about the toy it plays fetch with. Experimenting with different toys will help you determine which one it loves most. The instinct to retrieve is innate in your dog's genes. Fetching simply means go out, bring it back, and give it up.

How to Teach Fetch

1. Line up several toys and treats. Leave the food reward out of the picture.

2. Toss a toy your dog likes, a few feet away and point to it.

3. As it chases for the toy, encourage your dog to come back to you by reaching for the toy in his mouth and tugging on it. It will get the idea that bringing the toy back to you leads to a tugging battle. Eventually, you won't have to play tug every single time your dog fetches.

4. If your dog brings the toy back to you, shower it with praises but don't take the toy away.

5. If after getting the toy, your dog ignores you, pretend to eat some of its yummy treats.

6. Say 'bring' as your dog catches on and trots happily to you.

7. Toss a toy it likes most and go through the same procedure again.

Now that you are familiar with some of the advanced commands that you can teach your furry friend, you also want to learn a thing or two about making your dog social. We will learn all that in the next chapter.

CHAPTER 6

SOCIALIZATION SKILLS

Socializing for your dog is very important especially when you want to ensure that your dog is comfortable and well behaved around other people and animals. It's recommended to socialize your dog while he is young and continue socializing him all through his life to maintain the social skills.

Remember that in socialization sessions, everything seems strange to your dog. In this case, introduce everything to him in a calm reassuring way so he can adjust to the new world. Keep the exposure short to avoid overwhelming your dog.

There are several ways of socializing your dog, starting from inviting people to your home, to enrolling your dog for socializing classes. Below are some ways to keep your dog socially active.

Expose Your Dog to New Experiences and People between the Ages of 3 -12 Weeks

Dogs at the age of 3-12 weeks are more accepting to new experiences. During this time, expose your dog to as many, new but safe places as possible, i.e. to other animals and pets, vehicles, humans of all ages and sizes, and everything about outdoor life. Your dog's checklist of the things he should be exposed to is as follows;

- Children- in case you don't have kids at your house, take your dog to a park where he can meet children playing (bearing in mind if the park allows you to bring your dog with you). Take time with your dog there, so he can see and listen to the kids as they play.

- Unfamiliar people of different sizes, gender, and ethnicities- expose your dog to every type of people as long as they are willing to handle him in a positive manner. Let him come across people wearing hats, boots, and jackets.

- Other pets/animals- in case you don't have another pet in your house, take your dog to a dog park where he can safely socialize with other dogs. You can as well expose your dog to your friend's cat or any other pet by just sitting calmly next to them.

Consider Enrolling Your Dog for Socialization Classes

Socialization skills are offered at veterinarian clinics, community centers, and large pet stores. These classes aim to introduce your dog to many new experiences and sights such as people, other dogs, puppies, various sounds, smells, sights, and equipment. Your dog will be allowed off its leash to play with different people and other dogs. This will help your dog get to know other dogs and people.

Basic obedience classes go along with socialization skill classes since the dog is exposed to sounds such as contraction sounds, traffic, odd sounds through the use of discs, and many other sounds.

CHAPTER 7

TRAINING DOS AND DON'TS

Training a dog can be difficult for the inexperienced. However, for the persistent, it is a rewarding experience. The following dog training dos and don'ts will help you avoid common pitfalls while training your dog.

Do Find a Distraction Free Location

Always teach your dog new commands at a location that is free from any form of distractions. This will enable your dog to focus on learning. After getting conversant with the command, you can slowly introduce distractions.

Don't Assume Rewarding Your Dog for Good Behavior

Many dog owners are accustomed to rewarding their dogs during training but forget to reward the dog for continued good behavior. It is crucial to reward your dog after following commands like "stay" and "drop it", to reinforce their importance. Also, don't keep on rewarding the dog to do basic commands; instead, you should make the rewards sporadic then phase them out after some time. In so doing, you will not need to carry treats all the time to get the dog to do stuff. For instance, don't be giving food treats all the times; you can offer a quick pat, a quick praise or anything else that you believe the dog loves but be quick to reward him if you have to.

Do Use both Verbal and Hand Cues

Loss of hearing and blindness are common afflictions for an older dog. Using both cues can retain the capability of communicating with your pet even after losing his sight or sense of hearing.

Don't Plan Sessions Longer Than 20 Minutes

It's unfair to expect a young dog to concentrate on learning for a period of more than 20 minutes. Rather, find only 20 minutes to work with your dog on a daily basis. After he reaches maturity, his attention span will develop allowing you to extend the sessions as you wish.

Do Practice Commands At Various Locations

Young dogs cannot comprehend that "sit" and "stay" commands are universal. According to the dog trainer website, a "stay" taught inside the house, has a slight connection to a "stay" practiced in a backyard. In this manner, practice your commands in different locations so your dog can associate the command with your hand signals and voice rather than location.

Don't Use An Excited Voice To Earn Your Dog's Attention

Using an excited voice will help you get your dog attention, but it's not recommended to compete with your dog for his attention. Use a firm and calm voice to give commands without repeating the cue. This will enable your dog to be coming to you even after he sees something else that is more exciting.

DOG TRAINING

Do Reinforce Pack Behavior at All Times

Your dog should perceive you as the head of your house before you begin training. Don't do anything that portrays you as the weaker party in your relationship otherwise the dog will try to do anything he wants because to him, he is the pack leader. This means that you shouldn't be overly excited when you see him, or pamper him with lots of treats for stuff. To build that relationship, you will have to reinforce good behavior and constantly punish bad behavior. Ensuring that your dog is heeling while on a regular walk is one way of building that bond.

Don't Be Afraid To Take Your Dog to a Dog Trainer

Even though you have not enrolled for a standard 8-week obedience course, think of scheduling a few appointments with a dog trainer. A dog trainer will give you insight into your dog's mind making the training easier.

Do Stay Calm

Dog training needs a lot of positive reinforcements and patience. Don't yell at or hit your dog since you want loyalty and not fear. Also, don't repeat a command multiple times because this only teaches the dog that they will only have to respond after multiple repetitions. I know this can be hard but it has to be done otherwise you will have a hard time training the dog.

Don't Stop Until Progress Has Been Made

Many dog owners end up getting frustrated and stop training before their dogs learn to respond to commands. Dog trainers say this reinforces bad behavior in your dog making him think that acting up will get him out of training.

Do mind your body language

Dog's can easily decode your body language so be careful how you act around the dog when issuing different commands or instructions. You don't want the dog to misunderstand you. For instance, don't just hold the treats out in the open when telling the dog to something. You will need to hide some of the treats to make the training more exciting for the dog and the rewards more sporadic. Otherwise, the dog will see it as if they are being bribed to do something. You also don't want the dog to be too dependent on treats to follow commands. And if the treat is in the pocket, keep your hands out of the pocket to ensure the dog doesn't just associate your hands in the pocket with treats. Instead of associating the treat with the command, he will instead associate the treat with hands in the pocket and this is not what you are trying to teach. Make the dog keep guessing! In addition, ensure to treat the dog just about anywhere; don't have a specific place where you issue the treats otherwise that's the only place the dog will associate with treats. As such, move to different parts of the house and outside the house to give treats.

Do expand the number of commands you teach your dog

Learning is only exciting to a dog if you constantly teach him new stuff. Just like humans, once we have mastered something and can do it with ease, we get bored. This also applies to dogs. Dogs too can start getting bored with the same old routine. As such, you should train your dog new skills and commands to make your dog an all rounded canine friend who is just adorable for everyone who sees how the two of you relate. Some of the commands you can teach him include:

- ✓ Drop on recall
- ✓ Leave it
- ✓ Drop it
- ✓ Clicker training
- ✓ Retrieve over high jump
- ✓ Wait
- ✓ Heel
- ✓ Long sit down (5 minutes)
- ✓ Long sit (3 minutes)
- ✓ Focus
- ✓ Retrieve on flat
- ✓ Broad jump
- ✓ Stand for examination
- ✓ Heel free
- ✓ Long sit (1 minute)
- ✓ Go out
- ✓ Off the couch
- ✓ Sit on street corners

CONCLUSION

You have just learnt everything you need to train your dog. Always remember to reward your dog every time he does anything right. This is the most crucial part of the training. Treats keep your dog interested and helps cement your bond.

Bear in mind that some dogs are tricky to train and may need more training time. You need to exercise calmness and patience and never yell at your dog, as this will only cause problems in the end.

MY FREE GIFT TO YOU!

100 DOG Training TIPS

Tips To Train Your Dog

As a way of saying thank you for purchasing my book, I'd like to send you an exclusive gift that will help with your dog training skills. It will also help with training your dog.

100 Dog Training Tips is 100 quick and exclusive tips to transform your dog even more. Check it out and bring the best version of your dog out **NOW!**

I am giving you this **FREE BONUS** to thank you for being such an awesome reader and to make sure I give you all the value that I can in your mission to have a Happy, Obedient, Well Train Dog!

To get your **FREE** gift visit the link below and follow the steps & I'll send it to your e-mail right away.

www.dogtrainingkindlebook.com

DOG TRAINING

Thank you again for purchasing this book!

I hope this book was able to help you to understand how to train your dog properly.

The next step is to implement what you have learnt.

Finally, if you enjoyed this book, would you be kind enough to leave a review for this book on Amazon?

Thank you and good luck!

Other Books by Dan O'Brian

Puppy Training: The Complete Guide To Housebreak Your Puppy in Just 7 Days